BASEBALL PORTRAITS
Baseball in the Twentieth Century

By Thomas Crawford

Copyright @2022 by Thomas Crawford

All rights reserved. No part of this book may be reproduced in any form or by any electronic or mechanical means, including information storage and retrieval systems, without permission in writing from the publisher, except by reviewers, who may quote brief passages in a review.

This publication contains the opinions and ideas of its author. It is intended to provide helpful and informative material on the subjects addressed in the publication. The author and publisher specifically disclaim all responsibility for any liability, loss or risk, personal or otherwise, which is incurred as a consequence, directly or indirectly, of the use and application of any of the contents of this book.

WORKBOOK PRESS LLC
187 E Warm Springs Rd,
Suite B285, Las Vegas, NV 89119, USA

Website: https://workbookpress.com/
Hotline: 1-888-818-4856
Email: admin@workbookpress.com

Ordering Information:
Quantity sales. Special discounts are available on quantity purchases by corporations, associations, and others.
For details, contact the publisher at the address above.

ISBN-13: 978-1-953839-14-5 (Paperback Version)
978-1-953839-15-2 (Digital Version)

REV. DATE: 09/23/2022

BASEBALL PORTRAITS

Baseball in the Twentieth Century

By Thomas Crawford

For Mom and Dad and Alan

INTRODUCTION

Baseball evokes childhood, summer, sandlots, statistics, "Casey at the bat", Ring Lardner's "Alibi Ike" and, of course, The Babe. It is America's game and, I suppose, baseball means pretty much the same thing whether you are from Georgia, Maryland, Ohio or Texas. However, memories or visions of Major League players (whether seen or imagined at play) are shaped more by age than geography. Fans who grew up in the years 1900 to 1930 likely have vivid visions of Cobb, Ruth, Johnson and Mathewson. Fans growing up in the period 1930 to 1950 likely have their fondest memories of Gehrig, Foxx, Grove and Ott. Young fans of the post-World War II and racial integration years probably recall most vividly Williams, Dimaggio, Musial and Robinson. Fans born after 1965 may have particular affection for the likes of Mays, Aaron, Seaver, Koufax and Gibson but they can still relish the memory or vision of old-timers.

I grew up in Burbank, California, not far from the recently established Walt Disney Studio or from the slightly more distant Lockheed aviation plant, or the Hollywood Bowl. The population was about 60,000 and there were four movie theaters in a five block stretch along Glenoaks Blvd. My family lived and worked on an acre-and-a-half peach and plum orchard in the middle of a vibrant town. Baseball contributed to my blissful childhood. I grew up in Burbank before the Brooklyn Dodgers and New York Giants moved west of the Mississippi. Our "major league" was the Triple A Pacific Coast League and we lads of Burbank tended to support the Hollywood Stars (led by Frank Kelleher) at Gilmore

Field or the Los Angeles Angels (led by Lloyd Christopher) at Wrigley Field.

My first contact with the Major Leagues occurred in 1946 or 1947 when my Dad returned from a train trip to a Detroit automobile plant to purchase a DeSoto sedan and drove it home by way of Chicago, where he attended a game between the White Sox and Indians. At the game he met Bob Feller and obtained his autograph on a Rawlings baseball that he then presented as a gift to my brother and me. The thrill of that gift lasted until my brother's pitching hand wore away the idol's autograph.

Burbank's sole connection to the major leagues in post-WWII days was with the lowly St. Louis Browns whose team held spring training on Hap Minor Field at the Olive Avenue Recreation Center. In 1949 the World Champion Cleveland Indians (with Feller, Boudreau, Lemon, Rosen, Doby, Wynn, Satchel Paige, et al) came to town. I was asked to be the visiting team's bat-boy. With the exception of that experience fetching bats for the Indians, I knew the Major Leagues only from a distance by radio broadcasts and the Los Angeles Times sports pages. However, even following baseball from the remoteness of the West Coast was important to me.

Before high school and college, playing baseball ahead of other sports was the important thing. Our Burbank Braves baseball team played during the summer on the same Hap Minor field that the Browns did. During one winter league season our Blanchard Lumber Company teen team won the San Fernando Valley trophy with the coaching assistance of my best friend's dad, Don

Pulford, who had won 22 games in a season with the triple A Portland Beavers. Another friend, Mike Quint, and I made a sliding pit near my brother's pole vault pit in our back orchard to practice the techniques of Cobb and Robinson.

Neighborhood friends used to gather on our large front porch amid the Babcock and Hale peach trees and Santa Rosa, Mariposa and Satsuma plum trees laden with fruit. On hot summer days when we weren't doing chores or playing catch we played ping pong. Between matches we played a sort of baseball roulette board game. The game was played using pie-shaped templates placed over a spinner. Instead of the pie slices being red or black, odd or even, the templates were made up of numbered slices of various sizes representing base hits, walks and outs. Number "1" was a home run; '13" was a single; "7" might have been a ground out; and "10" was a strike out. Each template reflected the player's batting prowess. Thus, Ruth had an enormous "1" slice (and a shockingly large "10"). Cobb's combined base hit slices were greater than those of any other player, and, as I recall, Johnny Sain, a celebrated hitting pitcher, had a huge "13" to account for all the singles he had collected. Each participant drew or drafted one player for each position to make up a team and batting order. Then, spin on for as many innings as you wish.

My brother was a minor statistical wizard and enjoyed scoring games and poring over statistics. He used to listen to Fred Haney's broadcasts of PCL games at night and scratch on scorecards under the bed covers. I was not so obsessed, but I did collect baseball cards and write to favorite major leaguers for autographed photos.

Friends remind me that more than sixty-five years ago, teammates on our cub scout softball team scrambled over me to safety while I gathered up my spilt baseball cards from the floor of Mr. Holtzman's woody station wagon as it was perched precariously on the ledge off the road in Griffith Park. That road is not far from Chavez Ravine where the Dodgers play today.

My interests have broadened but the baseball memories and associations of my youth remain and please me, as may be true for most baseball old-timers, and the portraits in this little book reflect my appreciation for some of the most illustrious "boys of summer."

- Thomas Crawford

LIST OF PORTRAITS

Cy Young, 1867 14

Honus Wagner, 1874 16

Rube Foster, 1879 18

Christy Mathewson, 1880 20

Ty Cobb, 1886 22

Joe Jackson, 1887 24

Walter Johnson, 1887 26

Babe Ruth, 1895 28

Rogers Hornsby, 1896 30

Lefty Grove, 1900 32

Lou Gehrig, 1903 34

Martin Dihigo, 1905 36

Leroy "Satchel" Paige, 1906 38

Jimmie Foxx, 1907 40

Josh Gibson, 1911 42

Joe Dimaggio, 1914 44

Ted Williams, 1918 46

Jackie Robinson, 1919 48

Stan Musial, 1920 50

Yogi Berra, 1925 52

Willie Mays, 1925 54

Mickey Mantle, 1931 56

Hank Aaron, 1934..58

Roberto Clemente, 1934...60

Frank Robinson, 1935...62

Sandy Koufax, 1935..64

Juan Marichal, 1937..66

Tom Seaver, 1944..68

CY YOUNG

b. 1867, Gilmore, OH, d. 1955, OH.
6 feet 2 Inches, 200 pounds.
Pitcher, right-handed. Played with Cleveland (NL and AL), Boston (AL and NL), St. Louis (NL).

Cy Young won 511 games in a 22-year career, 94 more than the second - best total of Walter Johnson. His record will surely never be broken because pitchers today pitch at most every fourth day, and they are usually relieved before completing games they start. When asked about his endurance, Young reportedly said, "I just pitched every third day. Twarn't nothing to it."

Young pitched 76 shutouts during his career and his third no-hitter at age 41. In one fifteen-year stretch, 1891-1905, he won 414 games against 228 losses and had an ERA of 2.58. In 1955 The Baseball Writers of America created the Cy Young Award, given to the best all-around pitcher in baseball. In 1967 the award was bifurcated and given to the best pitcher in each league.

HONUS WAGNER

b. 1874, Chartiers, PA, d. 1955, Carnegie, PA.
5 feet 11 inches, 200 pounds.
Shortstop, right-handed batter.
Played with Louisville (NL) and Pittsburgh (NL).

Honus Wagner was barrel chested, bow-legged, long-armed and could play every position and is generally considered to be the greatest shortstop ever. He was so fast on the base paths and such a skilled base stealer that he was dubbed "The Flying Dutchman." He was one of the five initial inductees into the Baseball Hall of Fame, along with Ruth, Cobb, Mathewson and Johnson.

In twenty-one seasons he compiled a .327 batting average, collected 101 home runs, 1,732 RBIs, 3,415 base hits and 722 stolen bases. He led the National League in batting eight times.

RUBE FOSTER
b. 1879, Clavert, TX, d. 1930, IL.
Pitcher, right-handed.
Played with Cuban X-Giants,
Philadelphia Giants and Chicago Giants.

Rube Foster was a great pitcher who won 51 games in 1902 with the Cuban X-Giants and beat the Philadelphia Giants in the "Colored World Championships." The next year, having changed teams, he led that Philadelphia team to the championship. In 1910 he formed his own club, the Chicago American Giants. In 1920 he created the Negro National League and presided over its development as president. For his vision and acumen he is called the "Father of Black Baseball" and was elected to the Baseball Hall of Fame in 1981.

Honus Wagner called Rube Foster "the smoothest pitcher I've ever seen," and Foster reputedly taught Christy Mathewson the screw ball.

CHRISTY MATHEWSON

b. 1880, Factorville, PA, d. 1925, Sarana Lake, NY.
6 feet 1 inch, 195 pounds.
Pitcher, right-handed.
Played with New York Giants (NL).

Christy Mathewson was a great pitcher and a virtuous man of such perceived proportions that it is difficult to write a brief sketch about him. He was a star football player, class president and head of the literary societies at Bucknell College. In 1916 he left baseball and joined a chemical warfare unit in France during WWI. He was accidentally gassed, suffered lung damage and contracted tuberculosis which contributed to his death at age forty-five from tuberculosis pneumonia.

Mathewson and Walter Johnson are often judged by baseball historians to be the two greatest pitchers of all time. Mathewson pitched for fourteen years, Johnson for twenty-one; Mathewson won 373 games and lost 188 (a winning percentage of .665), Johnson won 417 and lost 279 (.599 %). A comparison of the best 15-year run and average reveals that the two greats had identical ERAs of 2.10, Mathewson had more wins and Johnson had more strikeouts. Statistics alone are insufficient to encapsulate a pitcher's greatness. Mathewson was known not only for his fastball but for his precision. He said, "A pitcher's speed is worth nothing if he cannot put the ball where he wants to. To me, control is the first requirement of good pitching."

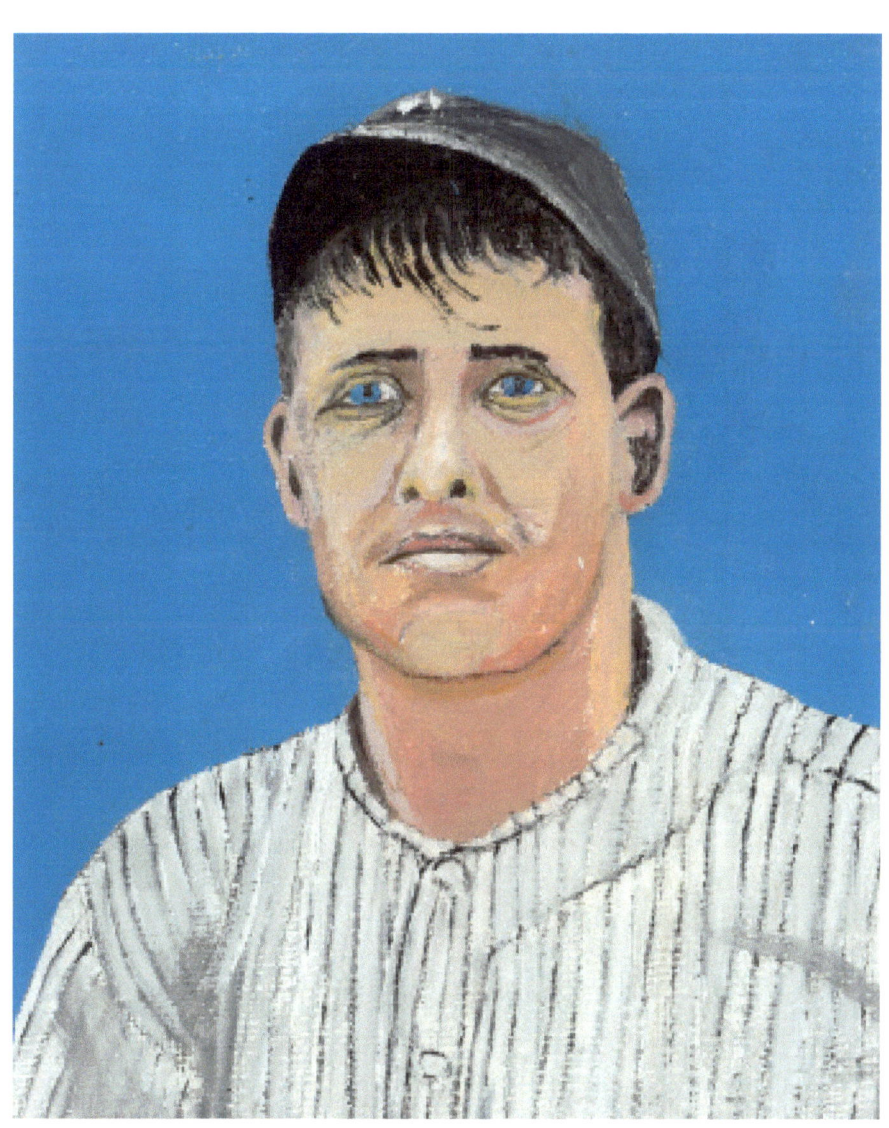

TY COBB

b. 1886, Narrows, GA, d. 1961, Atlanta, GA.
6 feet 1 inch, 175 pounds.
Center fielder, left-handed batter.
Played with the Detroit Tigers (AL).

Ty Cobb is indisputably among the greatest players of the twentieth century along with Ruth, Mays, Wagner, Hornsby and Gehrig and, reputedly, the most determined and fierce. He played 24 years and retired in 1928 after compiling the highest batting average of .367 (ahead of Hornsby's second best of .358) and scoring 2,246 runs (ahead of Ruth's 2,174). For fifty years he held the record for most career stolen bases, 891, until Lou Brock broke it with 938. (Brock's record was broken by Rickey Henderson in 1997 with 1,231).

An even more impressive statistic than Cobb's career batting average is his slugging average. Although not considered a power hitter, Cobb led the American League in slugging 8 times. Only Ruth (13 times), Williams (9), and Hornsby (9) led their respective leagues more than Cobb. Wagner and Musial followed Cobb with 6, followed by Mays and Foxx with 5, and then Aaron, Mantle and Frank Robinson, 4 each.

"SHOELESS" JOE JACKSON (shown with Ty Cobb)

b. 1887, Pickens County, SC, d. 1951, Greenville, SC.
6 feet 2 inches, 180 pounds.
Right fielder, left-handed batter.
Played with Chicago WhiteSox (AL)

Just as Ruth and Gehrig were the best power hitting teammates ever, Joe Jackson and Cobb could be paired as the best hitters for average playing in the same league at the same time; Cobb hit for .367, lifetime, and Jackson .356. In the 1911 season Cobb hit .420 and Jackson .404. Babe Ruth reportedly said that he modeled his hitting technique after Jackson's. Unfortunately, the brilliant batter's major league career was ended after ten years by the Black Sox scandal of 1919. Jackson was implicated (probably falsely) and banned from baseball even though he set a World Series record for most hits, 12, in that 1919 series in which he starred and ended his career.

WALTER JOHNSON

b. 1887, Humbolt, KS, d. 1946, Washington, DC.
6 feet 1 inch, 200 pounds.
Pitcher, right-handed.
Played with Washington Senators (AL)

Walter Johnson of the weak-hitting Senators of the American League is probably baseball's greatest pitcher, but Christy Mathewson of John McGraw's powerful Giants is very close behind. Ty Cobb said of Johnson, "He was one of the finest, most decent men in baseball, and he was too much a gentleman ever to dust me off at the plate although I deserved it."

In his career Johnson won 417 games with the Senators and lost 279 while opposing teams batted just .227 against him; he struck out 3,509 batters and had an ERA of 2.17. He won 25 or more games in seven consecutive seasons starting in 1910. In the 1912 season he won 16 consecutive games. In 1913 he had a 36-7 won-lost record and finished with a 1.14 ERA. In one especially notable four-day period in 1908 he pitched three shutouts in 3 games against the Yankees.

BABE RUTH

b. 1895, Baltimore, MD, d. New York, NY.

6 feet 2 inches, 215 pounds.

Pitcher, left-handed, Right fielder, left-handed batter.

Played with Boston Red Sox (Al) and New York Yankees (AL).

Babe Ruth is probably the most famous athlete in U.S. history and he is positively the best baseball player, not only because he was the best batter but also because he was a superb pitcher. Before being traded to the Yankees, Ruth pitched for the Red Sox for five years winning 94 games while losing 46. He pitched 29 2/3 consecutive scoreless innings in the 1916 and 1918 World Series. (A shutout record that stood for forty-three years). In the 1918 Series, the last one the Red Sox won in the twentieth century, Ruth pitched two wins.

Ruth's long-standing home run records (60 in a season and 714 lifetime) are known to nearly all baseball fans, here and abroad, but even more impressive are the surrounding details and statistics of his unequaled prowess. Ruth hit a home run every 11.76 at bats; Hank Aaron, who hit 755 homers, hit one every 16.7 at bats. In a six-year period from 1926 through 1931, Ruth hit 302 homers, an average of 50.3 per year. Twice, Ruth hit more homers in a season than any team in the league. His career batting average was .342. Perhaps the most remarkable statistic of all is Ruth's best five-year average for the period 1920 through 1924 when he averaged 38 doubles, 11 triples, 47 home runs and batted .370. Also, he averaged 138 walks against 83 strikeouts in that period. Ruth's phenomenal .690 career slugging average is 56 points better than the second best average of Ted Williams. He was walked 2,056 times, 35 times more than the second most feared slugger, Williams.

ROGERS HORNSBY

b. 1895, Winters, TX, d. 1963, Chicago, IL.
5 feet 11 inches, 175 pounds.
Second base, right-handed batter.
Played with St. Louis Cardinals (NL), and New York, Chicago Boston, all in (NL).

Rogers Hornsby was probably the greatest right-handed batter ever. His lifetime average over 23 seasons of .358 is second only to Cobb's .367. While playing for the Cardinals in the period 1921 through 1925, his five-year batting average was .402, which included the 1924 season when he compiled a .424 average, the highest in major league history.

Hornsby was a single-minded player. He told sports writer Robert Lipsyte, "Baseball is my life; the only thing I can know and talk about, my only interest." When he was asked what he did in the off-season he reportedly said, "I'll tell you what I do. I stare out the window and wait for spring." Underscoring his focus on baseball is the fact that at age 30 he was the player-manager of the Cardinals in 1926 when his team beat the New York Yankees in the World Series.

In addition to his .358 lifetime batting average, Hornsby hit 301 home runs in his career, the second highest after Ruth at the time of his retirement. Statistically speaking, Rogers Hornsby stands at the apex of epic batters; but he was not one of the most colorful stars.

LEFTY GROVE
b. 1900, Lanaconing, MD, d. 1975, Norwalk, OH.
6 feet 3 inches, 190 pounds.
Pitcher, left-handed.
Played with Philadelphia Athletics (AL)

Lefty Grove was probably the best left-handed pitcher of all time. He won 300 games against 141 losses, a percentage of .680. He led the American League in ERA 9 times, in strike outs 7 times and in winning percentage 5 times. He was the greatest nemesis of the Yankees' murderer's row." On one occasion he struck out Ruth, Gehrig and Meusel on 9 pitches. Another time he entered a game as a reliever with no outs and the bases loaded and he struck out Ruth, Gehrig and Lazzeri with 10 pitches.

LOU GEHRIG
(shown with Babe Ruth and Miller Huggins)
b. 1903, New York, NY, d. 1941, Riverdale, NY.
6 feet, 200 pounds.
First-base, threw and battled left-handed. Played with New York Yankees.

Lou Gehrig, the best first baseman and run producer in baseball, played in 2,130 consecutive games, a record until broken by Cal Ripkin in 1995. He batted clean-up in the Yankees order behind Ruth and was the all-time leader in RBIs with 1,995 in seventeen seasons until Hank Aaron passed him with 2,297 in twenty-three seasons. In one thirteen- year period, 1926 through 1938, he batted in 1,912 runs, an average of 147 per season. In 1927, the year Ruth hit 60 home runs, Gehrig had 175 RBIs.

Ted Williams considered Gehrig to be the second best hitter ever, after Ruth, and his career statistics justify that ranking: batting average .340, slugging average .632 (behind Ruth and Williams), on base percentage .447 (behind Williams and Ruth, and ahead of Cobb and Foxx). He drove in 100 runs or more, 13 years in a row.

MARTIN DIHIGO

b. 1905, Matanzas, Cuba, d. 1971, Cienfuegos, Cuba.
6 feet 3 inches, 220 pounds.
Pitcher, infielder and outfielder, threw and batted right-handed.
Played in the Negro leagues with Cuban Stars, Homestead Grays, and Hilldale Giants.

Martin Dihigo, generally considered the greatest non-North American player, was the first Cuban elected to the Baseball Hall of Fame. In Mexico he was called "El Maestro," in Cuba he was revered as the equivalent of Ruth or Dimaggio and called "El Immortal." John McGraw claimed Dihigo was "one of the greatest natural ball-players ever."

Dihigo was an overpowering starting pitcher who won 256 games against 136 losses. He played several infield positions and was a swift, graceful outfielder. In thirteen seasons he batted over .400 four times and had a career average of .304. Hall of Famer Buck Leonard, known as "The Black Lou Gehrig" said of Dihigo, "If he's not the greatest, I don't know who is."

LEROY "SATCHEL" PAIGE

b. 1906, Mobile, AL, d. 1982, Kansas City, MO.
6 feet 3 inches, 180 pounds.
Pitcher, right-handed. Played with Cleveland (AL) and St. Louis (AL);
And with several Negro Leagues teams, including Pittsburgh Crawfords, Homestead Grays, Kansas City Monarchs

Satchel Paige, like Babe Ruth, learned to play baseball in a reform school. Later, as professional ball players, what Babe the batter represented in terms of crowd appeal and gate receipts, Satchel the pitcher represented on the mound. His attraction was so great (and his appreciation for the rewards) that he bought his own plane and barnstormed around the country, summer and winter, pitching against local teams earning acclaim and money.

After playing more than twenty-five years in the Negro leagues, Paige became a 42 year-old rookie with the Cleveland Indians winning 6 games against one loss and contributing to the World Series Championship of 1948. He continued to pitch with the Indians and Browns to the age of fifty-nine. Accurate statistics are not available to confirm Satchel's estimate that he won 2,000 games and pitched 100 no-hitters. His fastball was only one of many, including his hesitation pitch, in his legendary arsenal. He was inducted into the Baseball Hall of Fame in 1971.

Satchel, one of the great linguists of baseball (along with Dizzy Dean, Yogi Berra and Casey Stengel), gave much good advice on how to stay young. For example, he counseled to "go very light on the vices, such as carrying on in society. The social ramble ain't restful."

JIMMIE FOXX

b. 1907, Sudlersville, MD, d. 1976, Miami, FL.
6 feet, 195 pounds.
First baseman, threw and battered right-handed.
Played with Philadelphia (AL) and Chicago (NL).

Jimmie Foxx was a powerful batter with huge biceps who could, reputedly, hit a ball as far and hard as anyone. Ted Williams said, "I never saw anyone hit a baseball harder than Foxx." When space scientists puzzled over an unidentified object found by astronauts on the moon in the 1970s, Lefty Gomez, a top Yankee pitcher quipped, "I knew immediately what it was...a ball hit off me by Foxx in 1937."

Foxx has the fourth highest slugging average in baseball history (.609), behind Ruth, Williams and Gehrig. He hit 534 home runs in his career and is the only player to hit 30 or more homers in twelve consecutive years. He is the fifth all-time leader in RBIs with 1,922.

JOSH GIBSON
(shown with Satchel Paige)
b. 1911, Buena Vista, GA, d. 1947, Pittsburgh, PA.
6 feet 1 inch, 215 pounds.
Catcher, threw and batted right-handed.
Played with the Homestead Grays and Pittsburgh Crawfords.

Josh Gibson was the greatest catcher ever, and after Ruth, the man called "The Black Babe Ruth" was probably the greatest slugger. Playing his entire career in the Negro leagues and winter leagues where major leaguers also played, Gibson had a lifetime batting average of .391 in the Negro Leagues and .412 against major league pitchers. One of Gibson's towering homers hit in St. Louis was measured by officials and found to have traveled 550 feet from home plate.

Walter Johnson said of Josh, "There is a catcher that any big league club would like to buy for $200,000. His name is Gibson... he can do everything. He hits the ball a mile. And he catches so easy he might as well be in a rocking chair. Throws like a rifle.... Too bad this Gibson is a colored fellow." At the time the Homestead Grays were paying him $6,000 a year. In 1972 Josh Gibson became the second African-American to be inducted into the Baseball Hall of Fame.

JOE DIMAGGIO

b. 1914, Martinez, CA, d. 1999, Hollywood, FL,
6 feet 2 inches, 193 pounds.
Center field, threw and batted right handed.
Played with New York Yankees.

Joe Dimaggio was not as great as Babe Ruth but he was almost as legendary. Popular musicians sang about him, Hemingway wrote about his aura of greatness in "The Old Man and the Sea," and after retirement from baseball he married Marilyn Monroe. His pride and self-assurance matched his superior ability. After a phenomenal season as a twenty three-year old, Dimaggio sought a $40,000 contract, a $25,000 raise over his previous contract. The Yankees' owner said, "Young man, do you realize that Lou Gehrig makes only $43,000 a year after 13 seasons?" Dimaggio responded: 'in that case, Mr. Gehrig is a very underpaid ballplayer."

Dimaggio played thirteen seasons (1936-1951) but missed three years, in his prime, to World War II. He is, perhaps, best remembered for his 56 consecutive game hitting streak of 1941. But his most spectacular season was his second year (1937) when he hit 46 home runs, had 167 RBIs, a .673 slugging average and led the league in runs scored, 151. None of his career totals of 361 homers, 1,537 RBIs, .325 batting average or .579 slugging average is in the top ten for those categories. But that does not detract from the power of his batting, the grace of his fielding or the majesty of his game, certainly not in the popular imagination of fans.

TED WILLIAMS

b. 1918, San Diego, CA, d. Inverness, FL,
6'4 inches, 205 pounds.
Left field, threw right-handed, batted left-handed.
Played with Boston Red Sox (AL).

If Ted Williams was not the greatest hitter ever, he was second best to Ruth or Cobb, depending upon one's bias. Williams played nineteen years but missed 3 years to World War II and 2 years to the Korean War because of military service. He finished his career with 521 home runs (20th best), 1,839 RBIs (10th best), .344 batting average (better than Ruth's .342), the highest walk percentage, .634 slugging average (second to Ruth's .690) and the best ever on base percentage at .483.

In 1941 Williams hit .406 and sixteen years later at age 39 he hit .388. Twelve times in his career he slugged .600; he led the league in on base percentage 12 times and in slugging 8 times. He hit a home run in his last at bat in 1960 when he was forty-two. Although Dimaggio consistently received more favorable press and fan appreciation than Williams there can be no doubt of Williams's superiority at the plate.

JACKIE ROBINSON
b. 1919, Cairo, GA, d. 1972, Stamford, CT.
5 feet 11 inches, 204 pounds
Second base, threw and batted right-handed.
Played with Brooklyn Dodgers.

Jackie Robinson was not as great a player as Babe Ruth or Josh Gibson but he was one of the greatest and he was surely the greatest all-around athlete to excel in baseball. He is to baseball what Lincoln is to American politics and social justice. When he broke the racial barrier in 1947, he became an international hero and saved baseball from itself.

Robinson was named Rookie of the year in 1947 at age 28. (most major leaguers debut by age twenty-one and play for at least fifteen years thereafter). In that first year he scored 125 runs, collected 125 hits, batted .297 and led the league in stolen bases with 29, (Pete Reiser was second with 14). Two years later Robinson was the MVP, winning the batting title with a .342 average, and had 124 RBIs and a .538 slugging average. His totals in his brief ten- year career were: 1,518 hits, 137 homers, 734 RBIs, 740 walks against 291 strikeouts, batting average of .311, on base percentage .410, slugging average .474 and 197 stolen bases. It is doubtful there was a more dignified or fierce competitor than Jackie Robinson.

STAN MUSIAL

b. 1920, Donora, Pa, d. 2013, Louis, MO.
6 feet, 175 pounds.
Left field and First base, threw and battled left-handed.
Played with St. Louis Cardinals.

Growing up in southern California after World War II when there were no major league teams west of the Mississippi, young fans like me followed Triple A teams of the Pacific Coast League, but we were keenly aware of the exploits of Stan Musial, Williams, Dimaggio and Feller. We paid attention to the comparison between Musial, who dominated the National League, and Williams, who dominated the American League. Like Rogers Hornsby, the greatest Cardinal of an earlier generation whose statistics approached Cobb's, Musial's statistics approached but were shy of Williams's.

"Stan the Man" Musial played twenty-two years and had a lifetime batting average of .331, hit 475 home runs, had 2,646 base hits, a slugging percentage of .559 and was the National League MVP three times. In 1946 he led the Cardinals to a World Series championship over Williams' Red Sox. In that year he led the National League in eight categories, runs, doubles, triples, homers (39), RBIs, on base percentage, slugging and average (.376). Musial's grace and dignity matched his prowess.

YOGI BERRA
b. 1925, St. Louis, MO, d. 2015, West Caldwell, NJ.
5 feet 8 inches, 194 pounds.
Catcher, threw right-handed and batted left-handed.

Yogi Berra was a great catcher and "bad ball" clutch hitter who played on more winning teams than anyone, including other great Yankees, Ruth, Gehrig, Dimaggio and Mantle. He also managed pennant winning teams in both leagues, the Yankees in the American and the Mets in the National. His World Series records will probably never be broken: he played on 12 championship teams, caught in more series games (75), and hit more series home runs (12). He played nineteen years and was the American League MVP three times and compiled 2,150 hits, 1,175 runs, 1,430 RBIs, 358 home runs and a career batting average of .285.

Yogi is fondly remembered for amusing (and sometimes wise) non-sequiturs, such as the following: 1, "You can observe a lot by watching." 2. "Baseball is 90 percent mental; the other half is physical." 3. "The future ain't what it used to be." 4. "I didn't really say everything I said."

WILLIE MAYS

b. 1931, Westfield, AL.
5 feet 11 inches, 180 pounds.
Center field, threw and batted right-handed.
Played with New York and San Francisco Giants (NL).

Willie Mays is one of the dozen greatest baseball players. Before his Giants moved from New York to San Francisco, Mays along with Mickey Mantle and Duke Snider represented the greatest trio of center fielders playing in one city at the same time. Red Smith, the revered New York Times sports writer, said everyone argued over who was the best of the three but "Mays by all odds was the most exciting.' He created excitement with 660 career home runs, 3,283 base hits, 2,062 runs, 1,903 RBIs, a .557 slugging percentage, 338 stolen bases and spectacular fielding.

From 1954 through 1958 Mays had one of the best five-year periods ever when he averaged 115 runs, 191 hits, 27 doubles, 13 triples, 38 home runs, 103 RBIs, a .328 batting average and a .618 slugging percentage.

MICKEY MANTLE

b. 1931, Spavinaw, OK, d. 1995, Dallas, TX.
5 feet 11 inches, 198 pounds.
Right field, threw right-handed, batted both left and right.
Played with New York Yankees (AL).

Mickey Mantle's promise as a rookie seemed unlimited and his accomplishments, when he was not injured, were epic. He was the greatest switch hitter ever. He hit 536 home runs in his 18-year career. (No other switch hitter, with the exception of Eddie Murray with 504, was even remotely close). Batting left-handed he was faster than anyone out of the box reaching first base. In 1953 batting right-handed he hit a ball over the left-center field fence at Griffith Stadium estimated to have traveled 565 feet. Batting left-handed, three years later, he hit a ball out of Yankee Stadium estimated to have gone even further.

In 1956, he won the Triple Crown, hitting 52 home runs, batting in 130 runs and averaging .353 while collecting a .705 slugging average. He topped that off with 3 home runs in a winning World Series against the Dodgers.

HANK AARON
b. 1934, Mobile, AL.
6 feet 180 pounds.
Right field, threw and batted right-handed.
Played with Milwaukee and Atlanta (NL).

Hank Aaron, the home run king who broke Ruth's "unsurpassable record" of 714, finished with a life-time total of 755. That epic achievement is slightly diminished in the view of some admirers because in the category of homers per at bat Aaron is only sixteenth among all who played. However, he is first in RBIs with 2,297, ahead of Ruth (2,211) and Gehrig (1,995), second in runs scored with 2,174 and third in total hits with 3,771. His average of 60 strikeouts per year is exceptionally low for a power hitter. His grace and proficiency at bat were matched by his superb fielding and base running.

ROBERTO CLEMENTE

b. 1934, Carolina, Puerto Rico, d. 1972, San Juan, Puerto Rico.
5 feet 11 inches, 170 pounds.
Right field, threw and batted right-handed.
Played with Pittsburgh Pirates (NL).

Roberto Clemente, the greatest Puerto Rican ball-player, is also justly honored for his altruism. He was killed when on a relief plane that was overladen with emergency aid and medical supplies bound for Nicaragua crashed.

Clemente won four batting titles, had a .317 lifetime average and collected 3,000 hits. However, he lagged slightly behind his four greatest contemporaries. Aaron, Mays, Mantle and Frank Robinson in the power and run-producing categories of home runs, RBIs and slugging percentage. Many critics claim that Clemente was the greatest right fielder ever. He covered the field superbly, had a rifle arm and won twelve Golden Glove awards.

FRANK ROBINSON

b. 1935, Beaumont, TX, d. 2019, Los Angeles, CA.
6 feet 1 inch, 195 pounds.
Right field and first Base, threw right-handed, batted both left and right.
Played with Cincinnati (NL), Baltimore (AL), Los Angeles (NL), California (AL),
Cleveland (AL).

In Frank Robinson's first year in the major leagues he tied Wally Berger's rookie record with 38 home runs and led the league in runs scored. He is the only player to win the Most Valuable Player award in both leagues; he hit 586 home runs, fifth best all-time; and was the first African-American manager in the majors.

Frank Robinson consistently played at the highest level worthy of one of baseball's greats, and his 1962 season with Cincinnati is particularly spectacular. He hit 39 homers, had 136 RBIs, a .342 average, and led the league in runs, doubles and base hits. Moving to the American League in 1966 he batted clean-up for Baltimore and led them to three successive pennant years 1969-1971. One of his teammates, Pete Rose, said he never saw anyone prepare harder than Frank Robinson.

SANDY KOUFAX

b. 1935, Brooklyn, NY.
6 feet 2 inches, 210 pounds.
Pitcher, left-handed.
Played with Brooklyn Dodgers and Los Angeles Dodgers.

Sandy Koufax played only twelve years (1955 through 1966) before retiring because of arthritis in his pitching arm. It has been said that his first six years were mediocre (though in 1959 he tied Bob Feller's record of 18 strikeouts in 9 innings). However, from 1961 through 1966 he was magnificent, as indicated by the following stats: 1961, W-L, 18-13, 269 strikeouts; 1962, W-L, 14-7, 2.54 ERA (best in league); 1963, W-L, 25-5, 306 strikeouts, 11 shutouts and ERA of 1.88, (In the World Series he won Games One and Four, striking out a record fifteen batters); 1964, W-L, 19-5, led league in ERA and had seven shutouts; 1965, 26-8 and pitched his fourth career no-hitter; 1966, W-L, 27-9, ERA 1.71.

Throughout Koufax's career the Dodgers had an inferior offense. Los Angeles Times sports writer Jim Murray said, "What makes Sandy Koufax so great is the same thing that made Walter Johnson great, the team behind him is the ghastliest scoring team in history...With the Babe Ruth Yankees Koufax would have been the first undefeated pitcher in history."

JUAN MARICHAL
b. 1937, Laguna Verde, Dominican Republic.
6 feet, 195 pounds.
Pitcher, right-handed.
Played with San Francisco Giants.

Juan Marichal, the Dominican Republic's most valuable gift to baseball, seemed to be under-appreciated, at least by those dispensing awards. In the 1960s he won 25 games in each of three seasons and won a total of 191, more than anyone else, but never won the Cy Young Award. One can make the case that he was the best pitcher of his time by comparing the ten-year run average of the three best. Marichal's period (1962-72) produced 202 wins and 97 losses, a .675% with 1,940 strike outs (194/year) and an ERA of 2.64; Sandy Koufax (1957-66) had 161 wins and 81 losses a .665% with 2,336 strikeouts (234/year) and an ERA of 2.70; Bob Gibson (1963-72) 191 wins and 105 losses, a .645%, with 2,295 strikeouts (230/year) and an ERA of 2.65.

Marichal's high kick unnerved batters but did not hinder his control. In fact, Marichal's control was probably better than that of the pin-point pitcher, Greg Maddux, who walked 609 batters in 2,598 innings pitched, an average of 4.26 per inning. Marichal walked 709 batters in 3,509 innings, an average of one every 4.26 innings pitched.

TOM SEAVER

b. 1944, Fresno, CA.
6 feet 1 inch, 206 pounds.
Pitcher, right-handed.
Played with New York (NL), Cincinnati (NL), Chicago (AL).

Tom Seaver was probably the best pitcher of the last half of the twentieth century. He won 311 games against 205 losses, a .603 winning percentage, playing for teams whose winning percentage was .502. He was fourth all-time in strikeouts, with 3,640, and seventh in shutouts with 61. His career ERA was 2.86.

Seaver's best ten-year run average was in the period 1969-78. He won 187 games and lost 102 for a percentage of .647, struck out 2,381 and had an ERA of 2.52. Seaver's best ten-year average compares favorably to Walter Johnson's best period 1910-1919 whose numbers were 265 wins and 143 losses for a .650 percentage, with 2,219 strikeouts and an ERA of 1.72.

www.ingramcontent.com/pod-product-compliance
Lightning Source LLC
Chambersburg PA
CBHW042054050526
44107CB00109B/1125